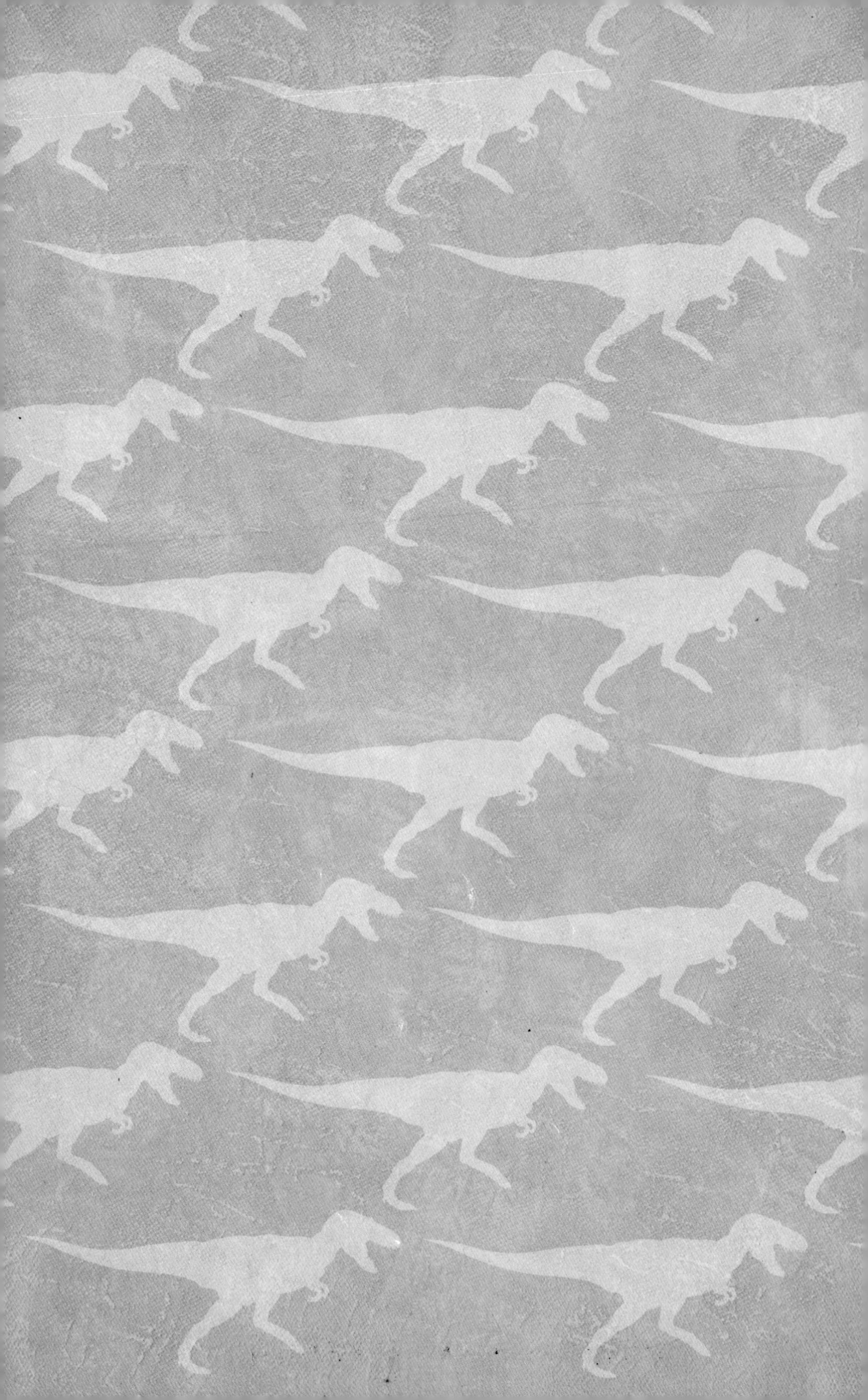

TYRANNOSAURUS REX:
MIGHTY MEAT-EATER

by Sheila Hammer   illustrated by Jason Dove

CONSULTANT:

MATHEW J. WEDEL, PhD
PALEONTOLOGIST AND ASSISTANT PROFESSOR
WESTERN UNIVERSITY OF HEALTH SCIENCES, POMONA, CALIFORNIA

CAPSTONE PRESS
a capstone imprint

First Graphics are published by Capstone Press,
1710 Roe Crest Drive, North Mankato, Minnesota 56003.
www.capstonepub.com

 Books published by Capstone Press are manufactured with paper
containing at least 10 percent post-consumer waste.

Library of Congress Cataloging-in-Publication Data
Hammer, Sheila.
  Tyrannosaurus rex : mighty meat-eater / by Sheila Hammer.
    p. cm.—(First graphics. Dinosaurs)
  Includes bibliographical references and index.
Summary: "In graphic novel format, text and illustrations present Tyrannosaurus
rex, its characteristics and probable behavior, and information about extinction"—
Provided by publisher.
  ISBN 978-1-4296-7602-1 (library binding)
  ISBN 978-1-4296-7932-9 (paperback)
  1. Tyrannosaurus rex—Juvenile literature. I. Dove, Jason. II. Title.

QE862.S3H36 2012
567.912'9—dc23

                    2011036564

EDITOR: LORI SHORES
DESIGNER: LORI BYE
ART DIRECTOR: NATHAN GASSMAN
PRODUCTION SPECIALIST: KATHY MCCOLLEY

Printed in the United States of America in Stevens Point, Wisconsin.
102011   006404WZS12

TABLE OF CONTENTS

KING OF THE DINOSAURS

The ground shakes. A terrible roar fills the air.

Animals flee in terror as Tyrannosaurus rex bursts through the trees.

AGE OF THE DINOSAURS

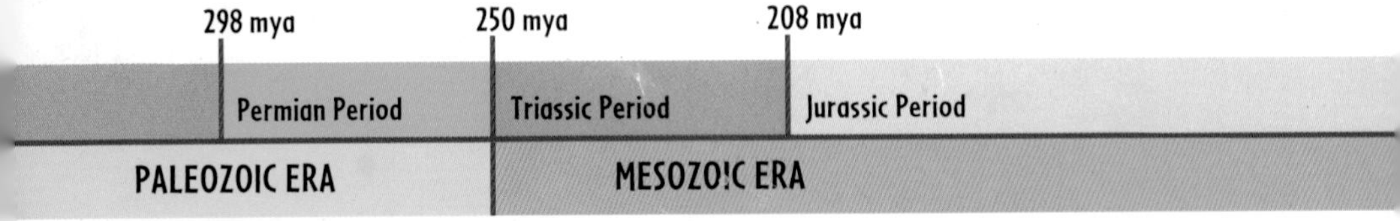

	298 mya		250 mya		208 mya	
		Permian Period		Triassic Period		Jurassic Period
PALEOZOIC ERA				MESOZOIC ERA		

T. rex follows its prey with large, forward-looking eyes.

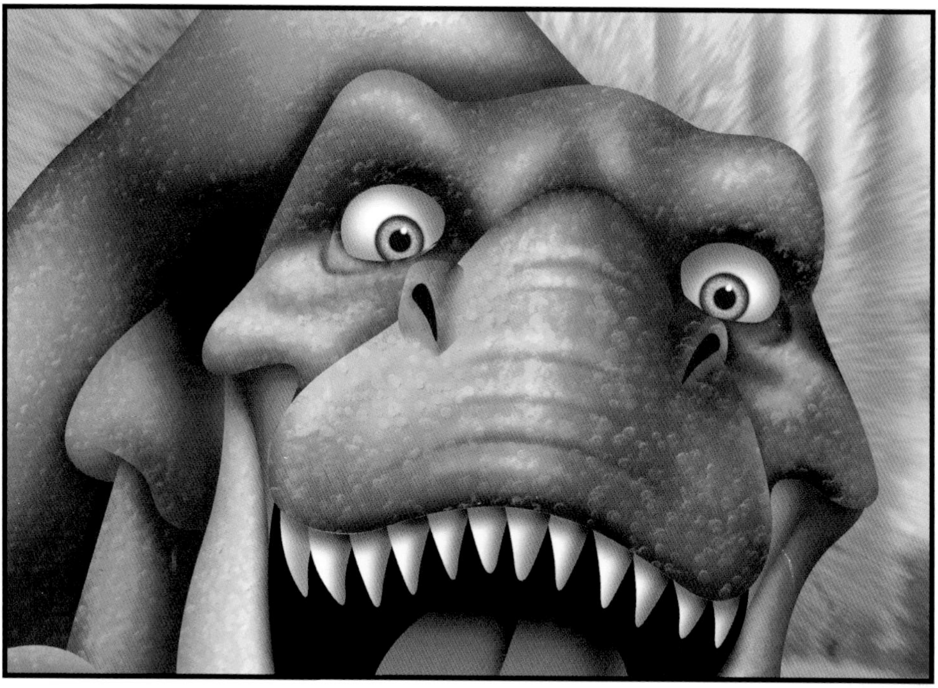

The giant predator easily catches weak and young dinosaurs.

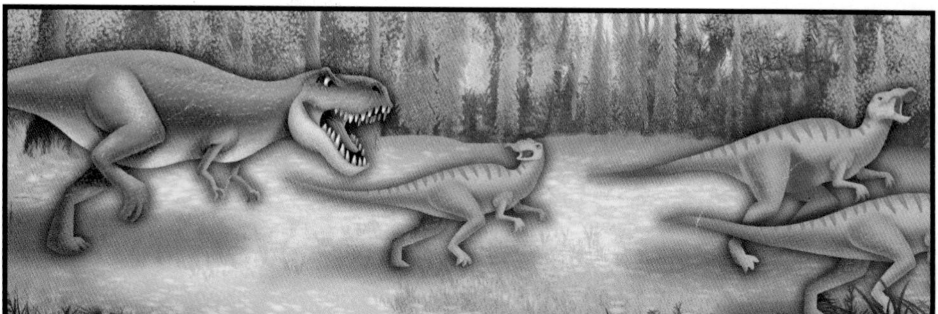

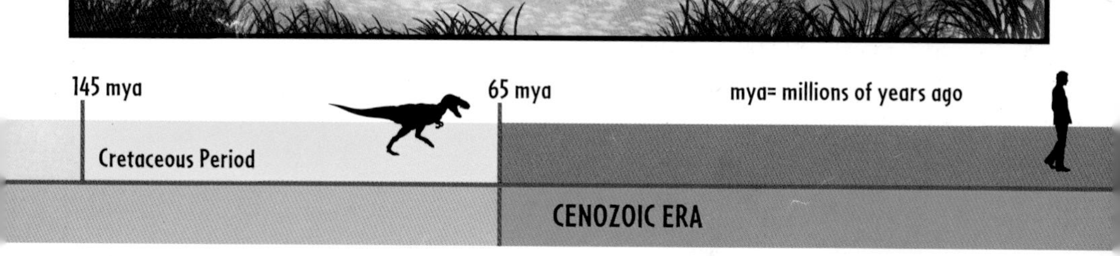
145 mya
65 mya
mya= millions of years ago
Cretaceous Period
CENOZOIC ERA

T. rex was the largest meat-eating dinosaur to ever live.

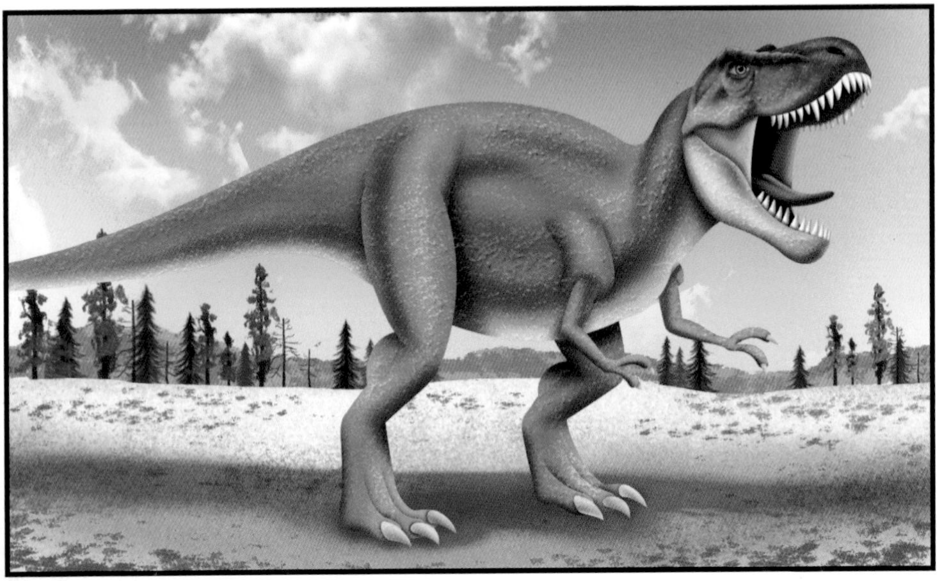

At 40 feet (12 meters), T. rex was longer than a school bus.

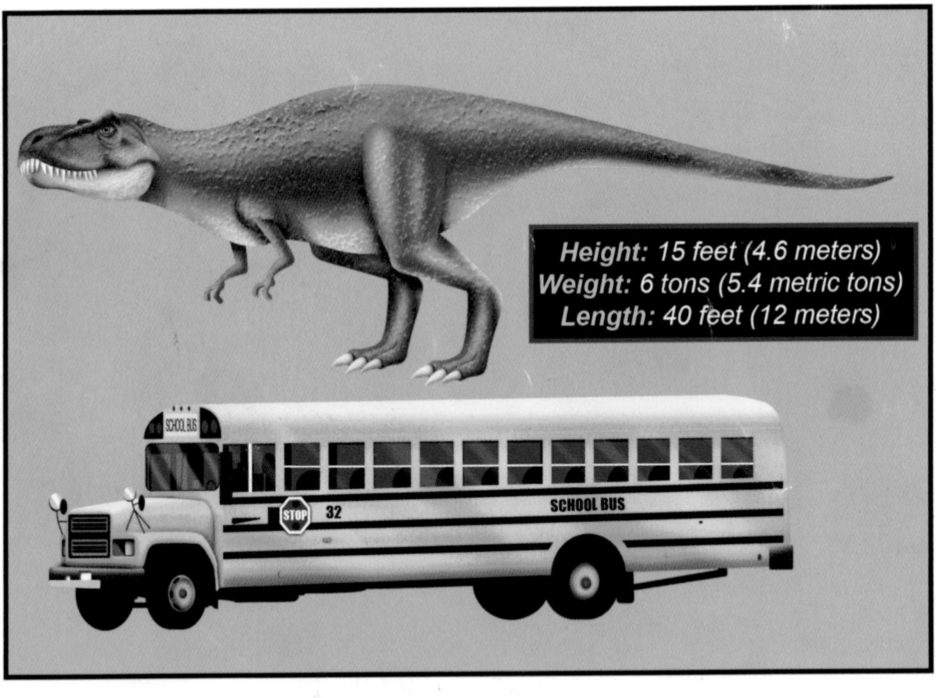
Height: 15 feet (4.6 meters)
Weight: 6 tons (5.4 metric tons)
Length: 40 feet (12 meters)
SCHOOL BUS
STOP
32
SCHOOL BUS

T. rex balanced its body over its legs like a teeter-totter. Its tail kept it from falling forward.

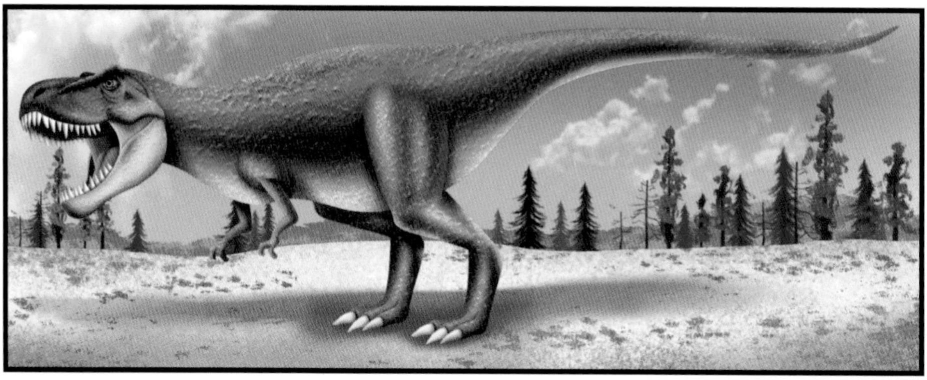

T. rex had strong arms with two fingers on each hand.

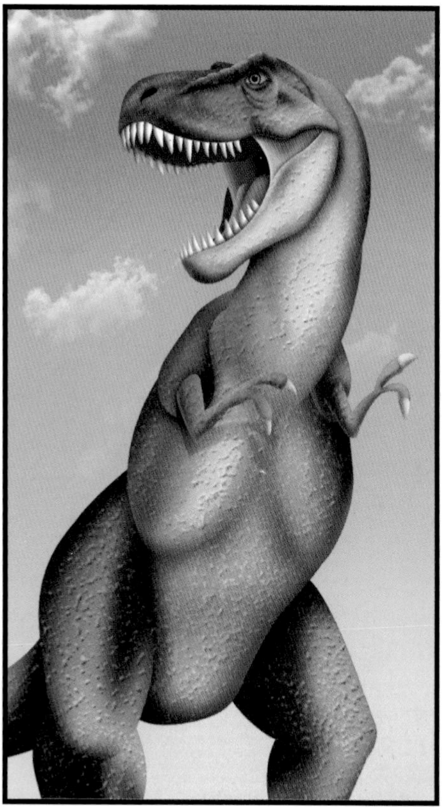

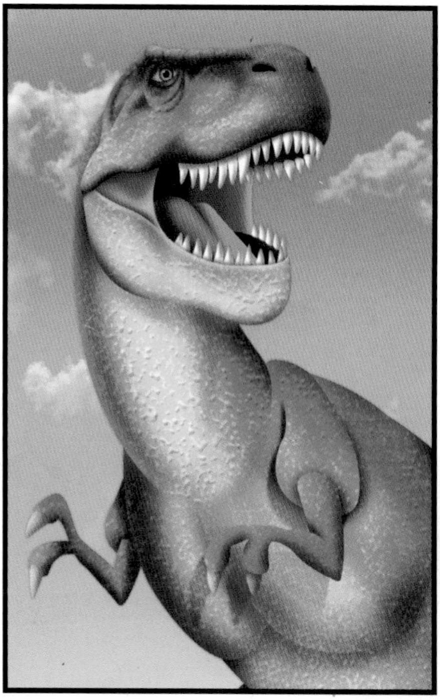

Large holes in T. rex's head carried sound to its brain. T. rex heard other dinosaurs far away.

Millions of years ago, T. rex lived in North America and eastern Asia.

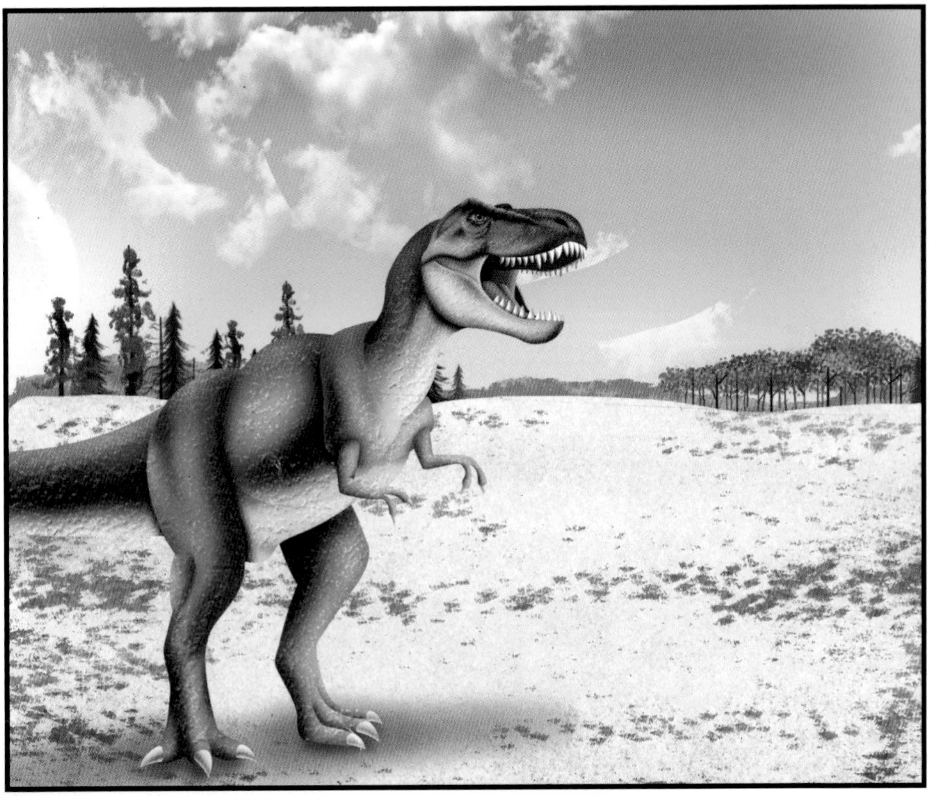

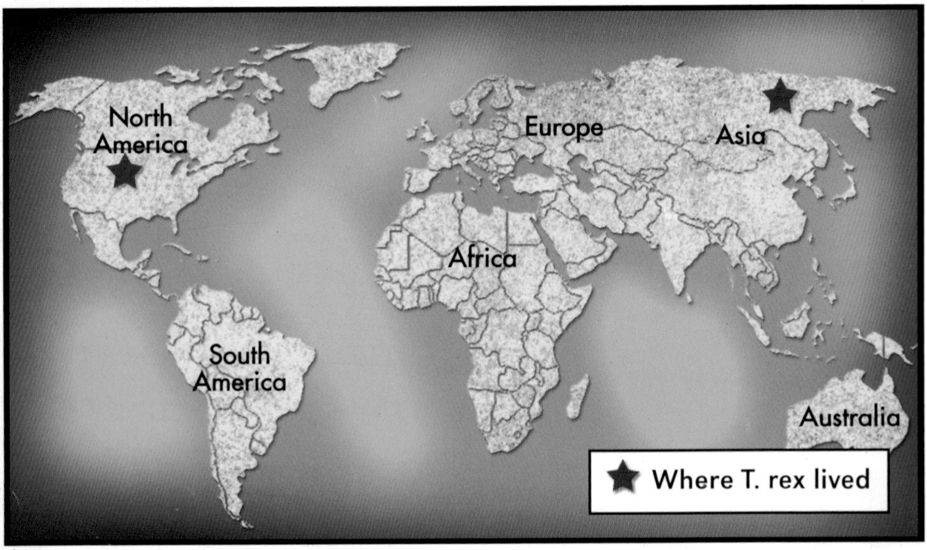
North America
Europe
Asia
Africa
South America
Australia
Where T. rex lived

T. rex lived in warm forests. Forests were also home to many plant-eating dinosaurs.

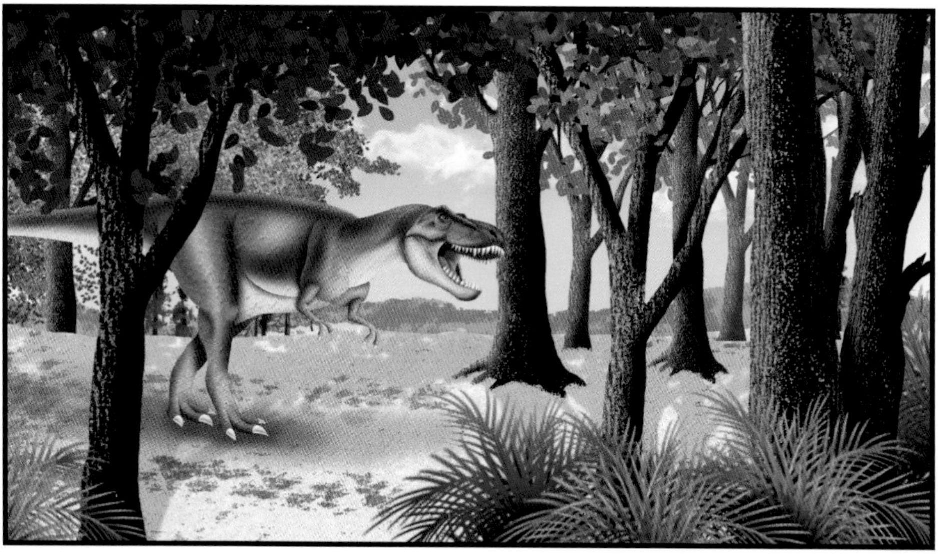

During T. rex's time, more types of dinosaurs roamed the Earth than at any other time.

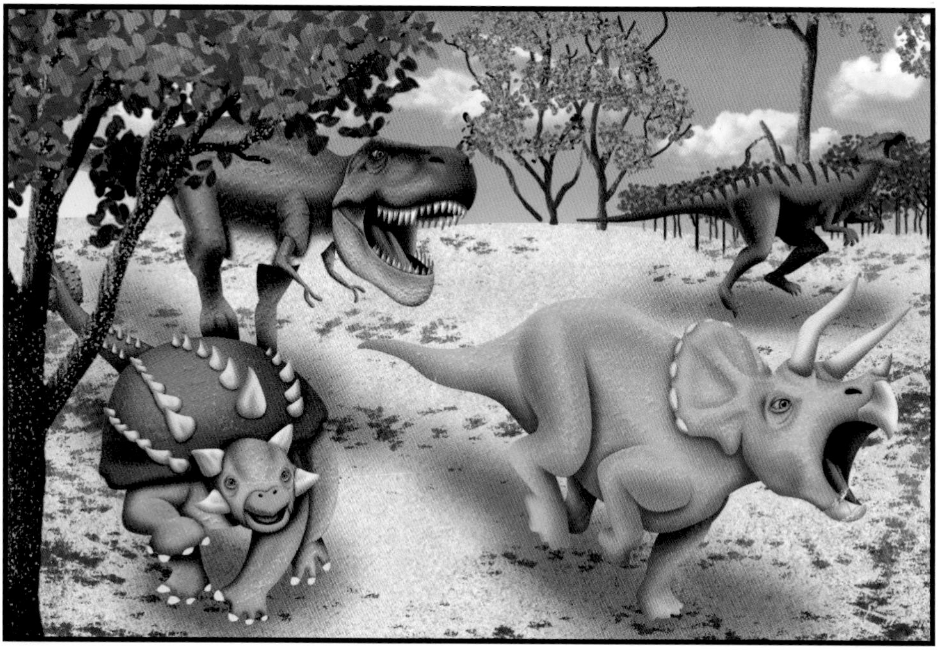

T. REX IS HUNGRY

T. rex moved its big head from side to side and sniffed the air. It smelled food miles away.

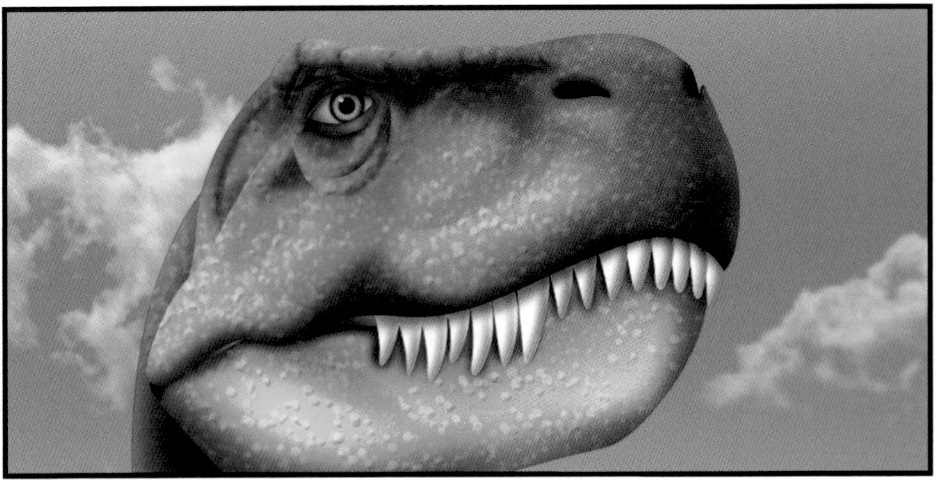

T. rex prowled through the trees. Each step was 12 to 15 feet (3.7 to 4.6 m) long.

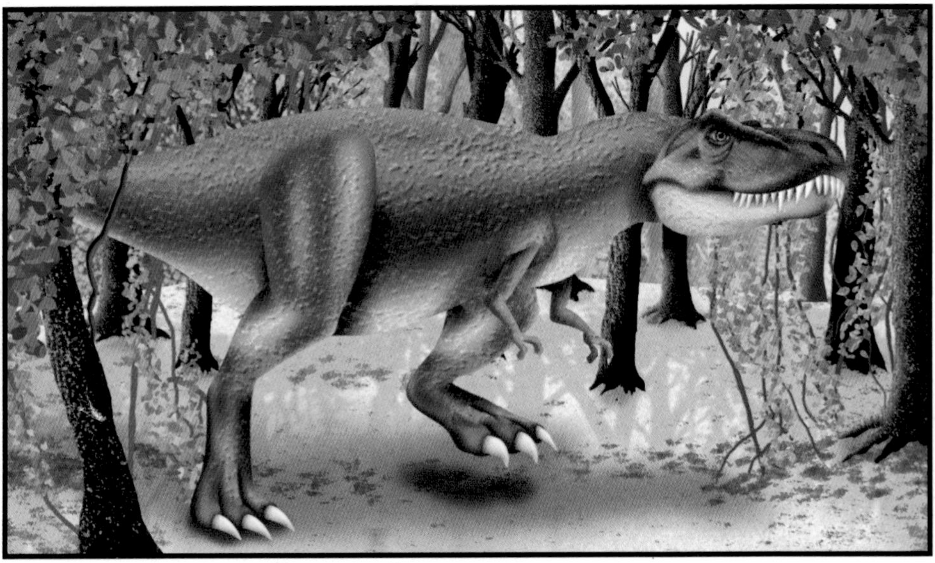

T. rex walked on the toes of its birdlike feet. Large claws tore up the ground.

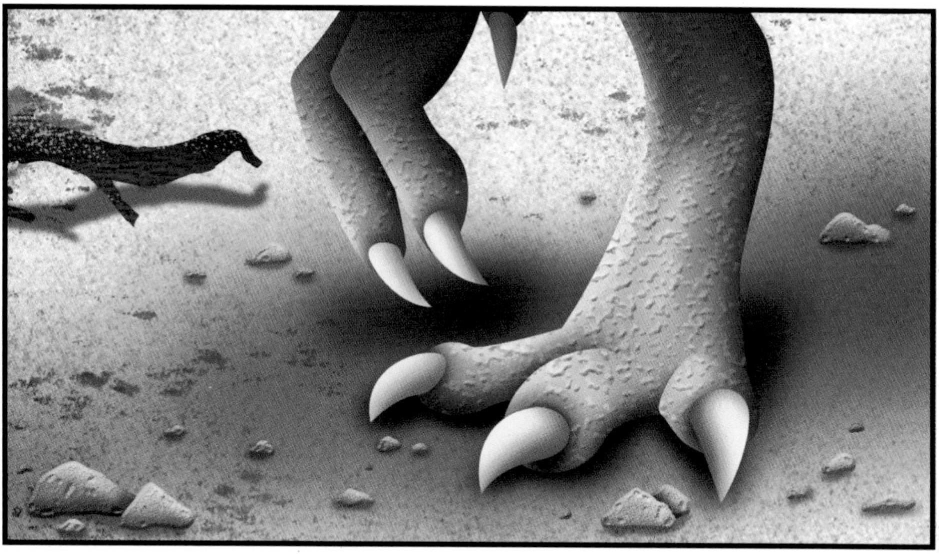

T. rex was also a scavenger. With a roar, it charged in to steal a kill.

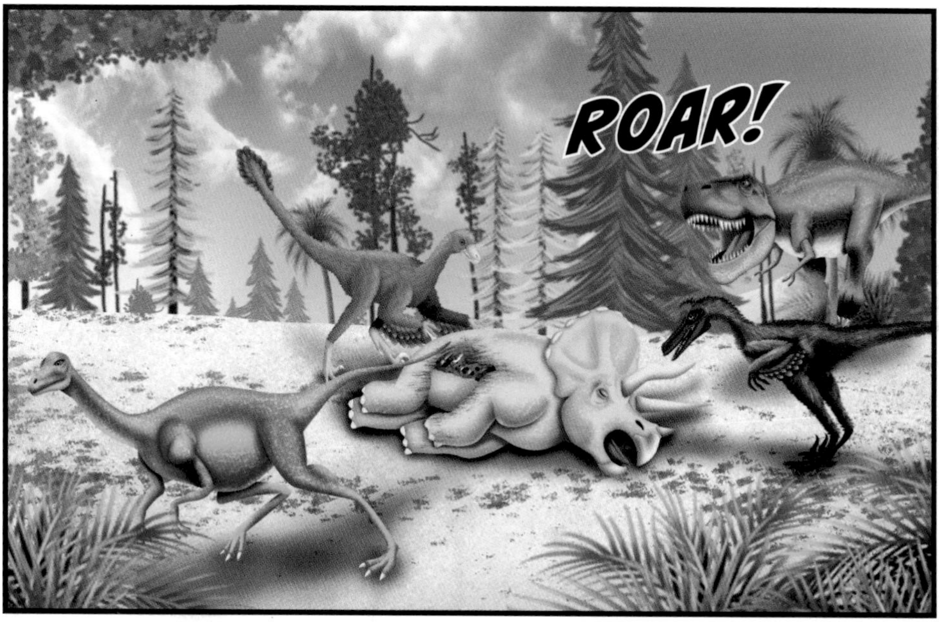
ROAR!

T. rex's huge jaws could tear off 500 pounds (227 kilograms) of meat in one bite.

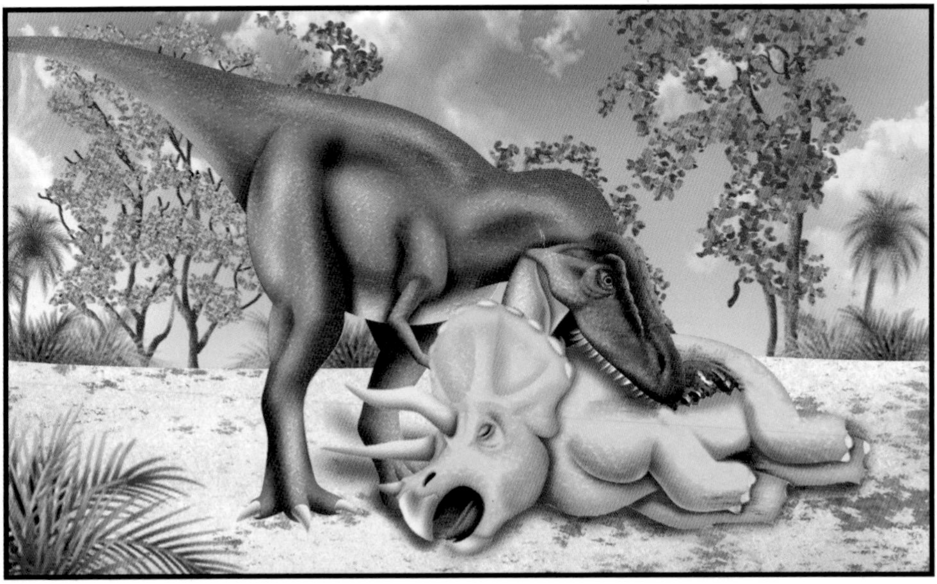

T. rex teeth were hard, sharp, and rough like a saw. Each tooth was about the size of a banana.

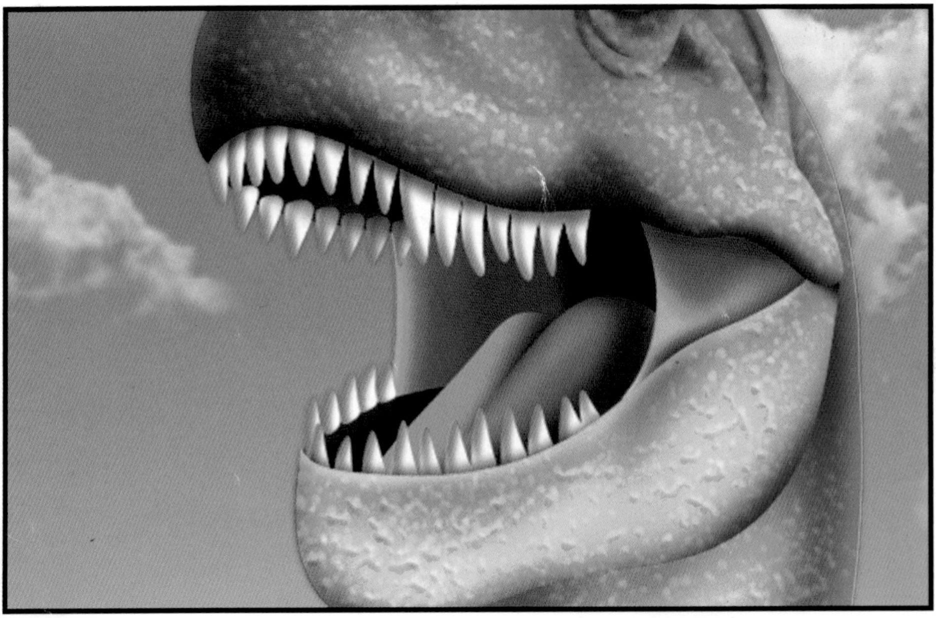

T. rex gobbled down both meat and bones.

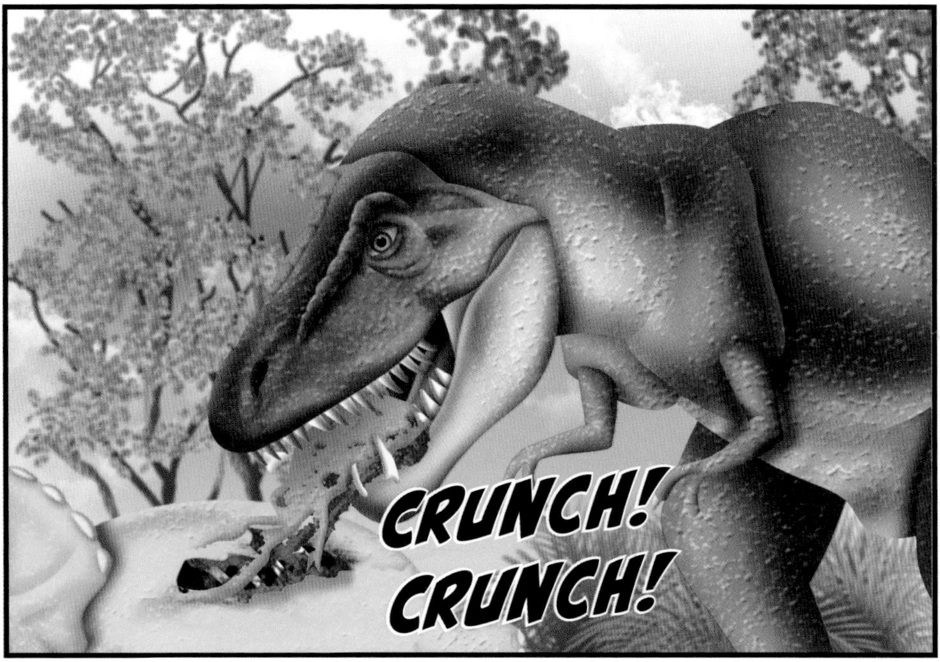
CRUNCH!
CRUNCH!

Some reptiles ate only one big meal every few weeks or months. But T. rex was warm-blooded and needed to eat every day.

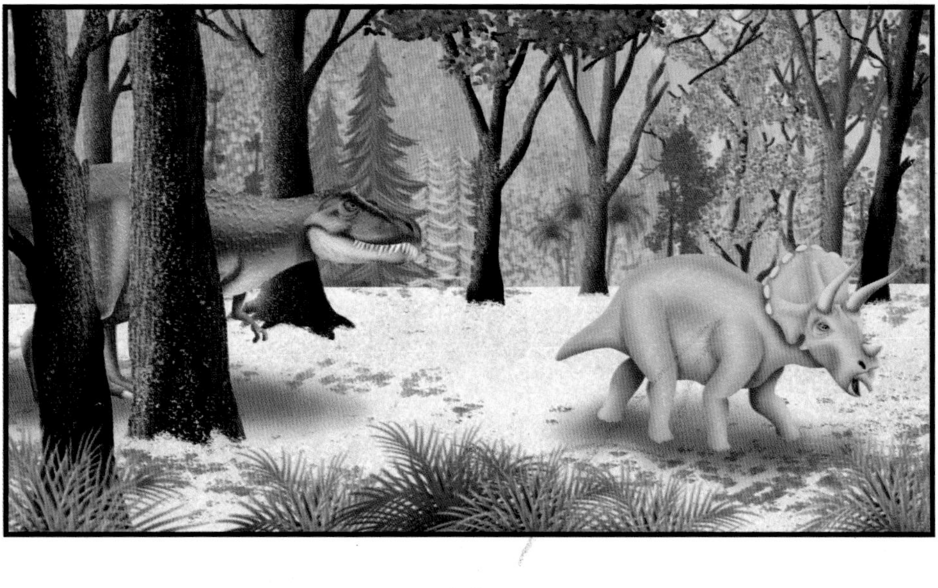

T. REX STARTS A FAMILY

Like other dinosaurs, a female T. rex laid eggs.

Baby T. rexes were born with feathered skin.
They had long and narrow heads.

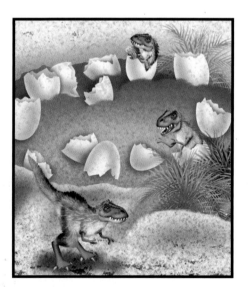

T. rex babies' long legs were built for running.
They ran quickly to stay safe.

Until they could hunt, young T. rexes relied on adults for food.

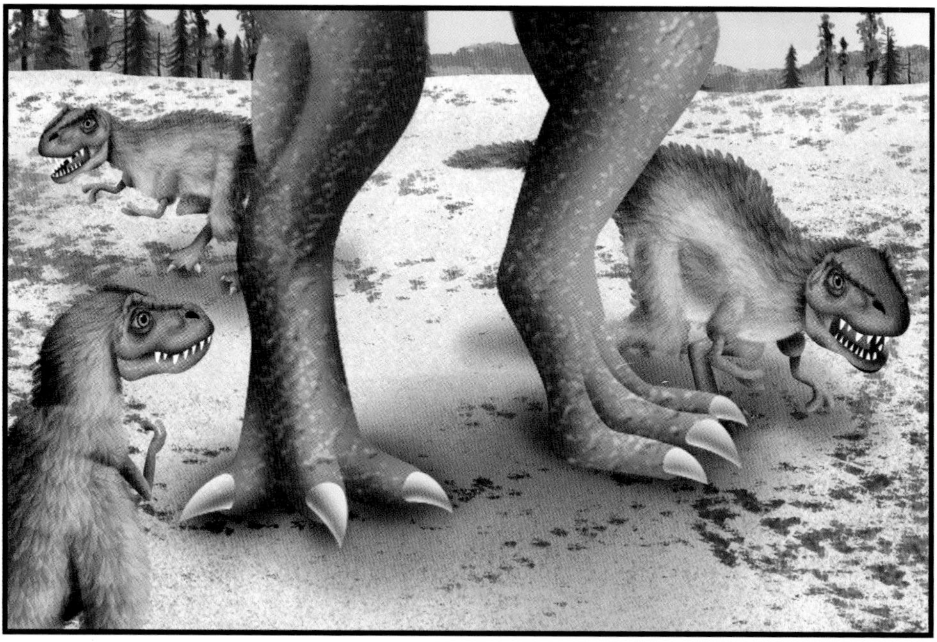

In 20 years, a young T. rex was fully grown.

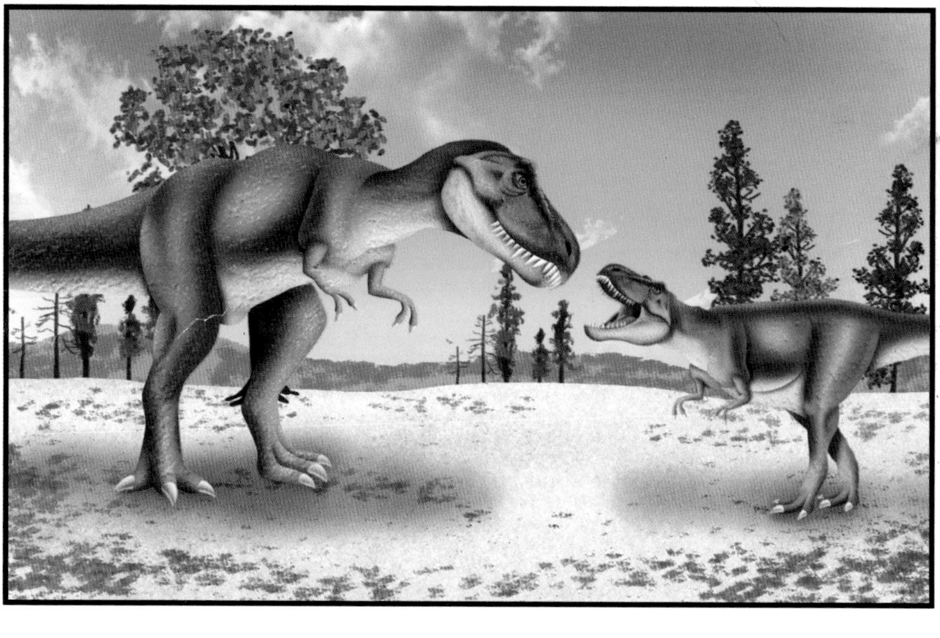

THE END OF THE KING

T. rex was one of the last large dinosaurs to live on Earth. All the giant dinosaurs died 65 million years ago.

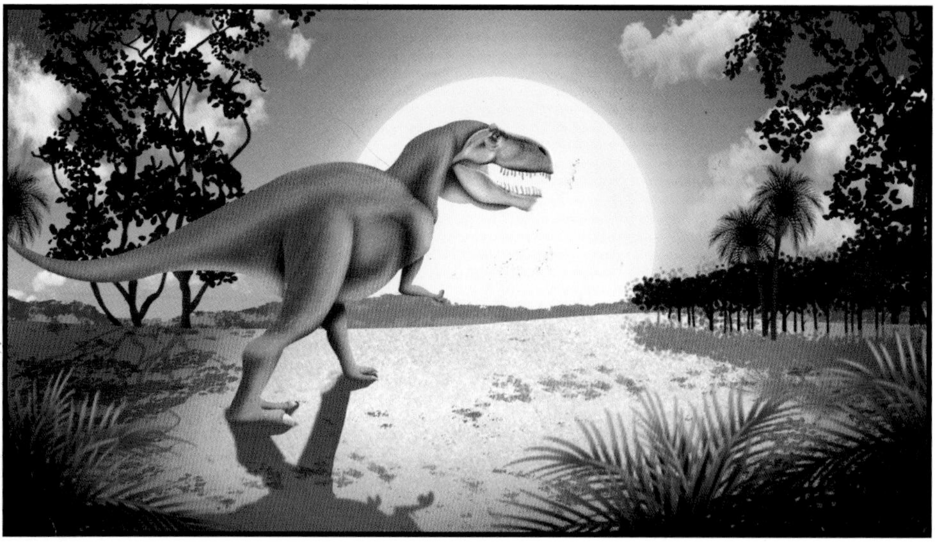

Scientists believe the dinosaurs died when a giant meteorite crashed into Earth.

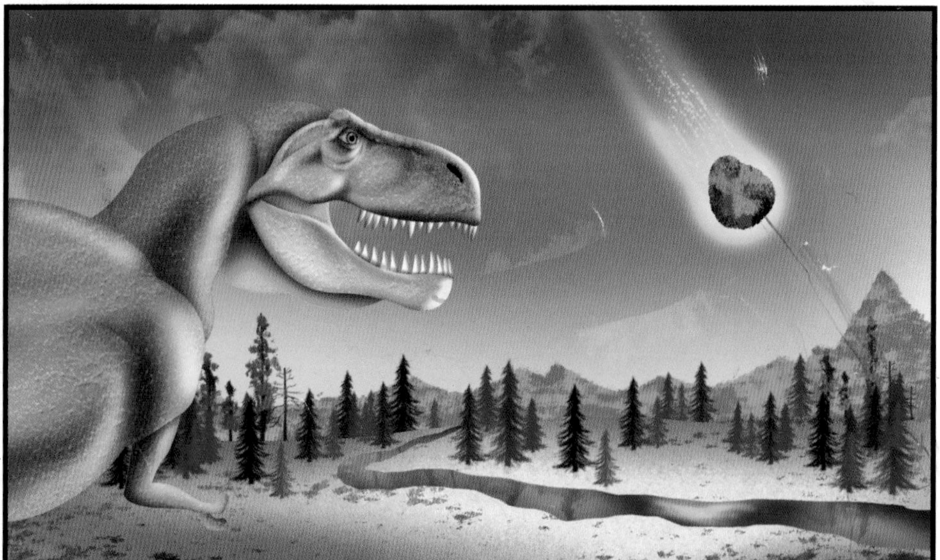

The meteorite caused a huge wildfire. The dinosaurs' watering holes dried up.

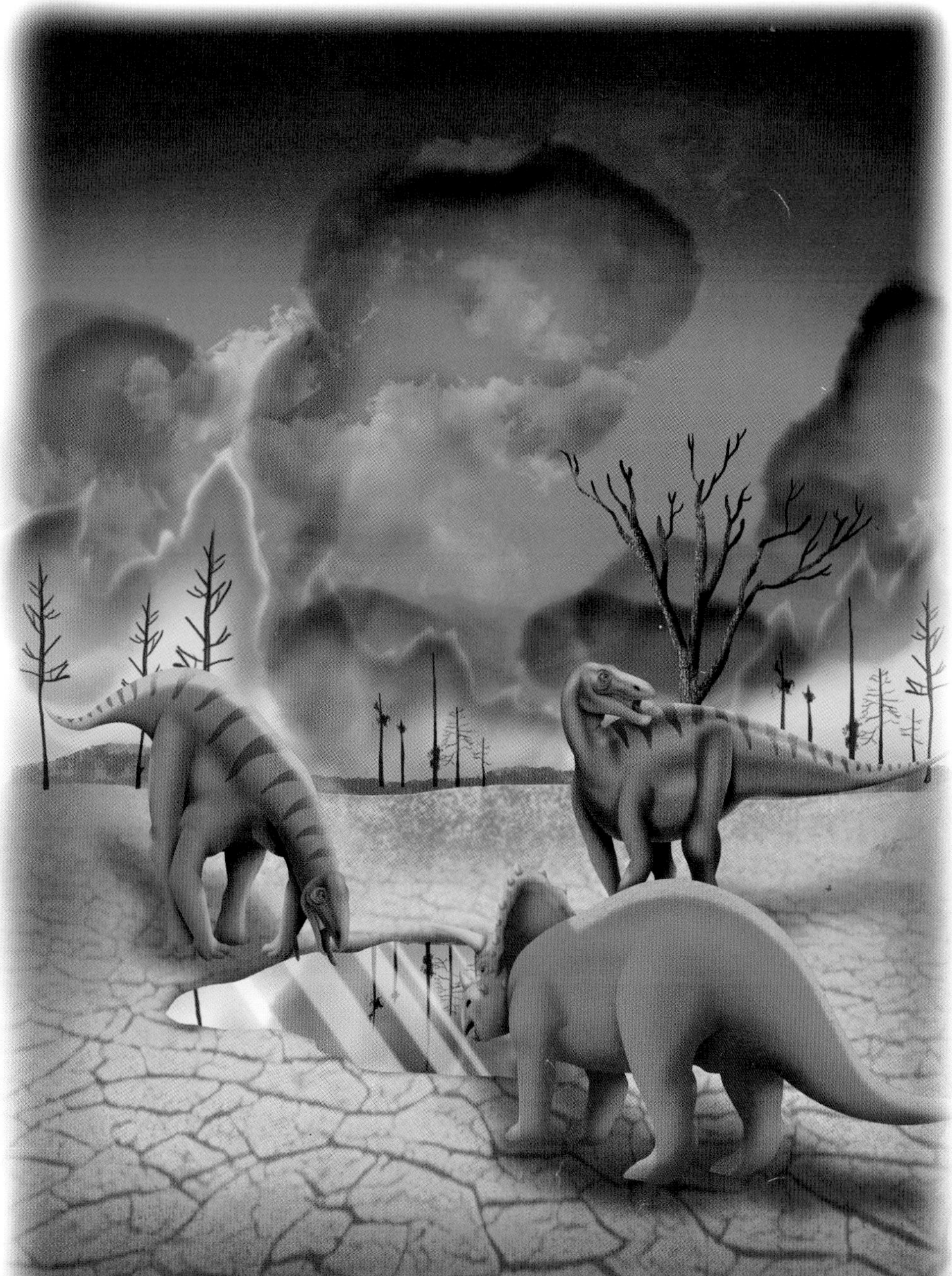

Dust from the meteorite hid the sun for years.

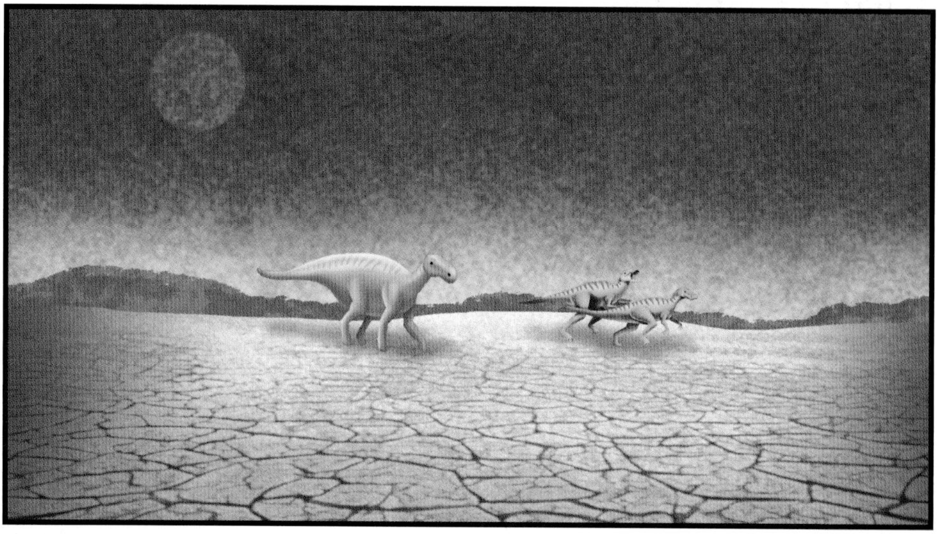

Plants died. Dinosaurs had a hard time finding food.

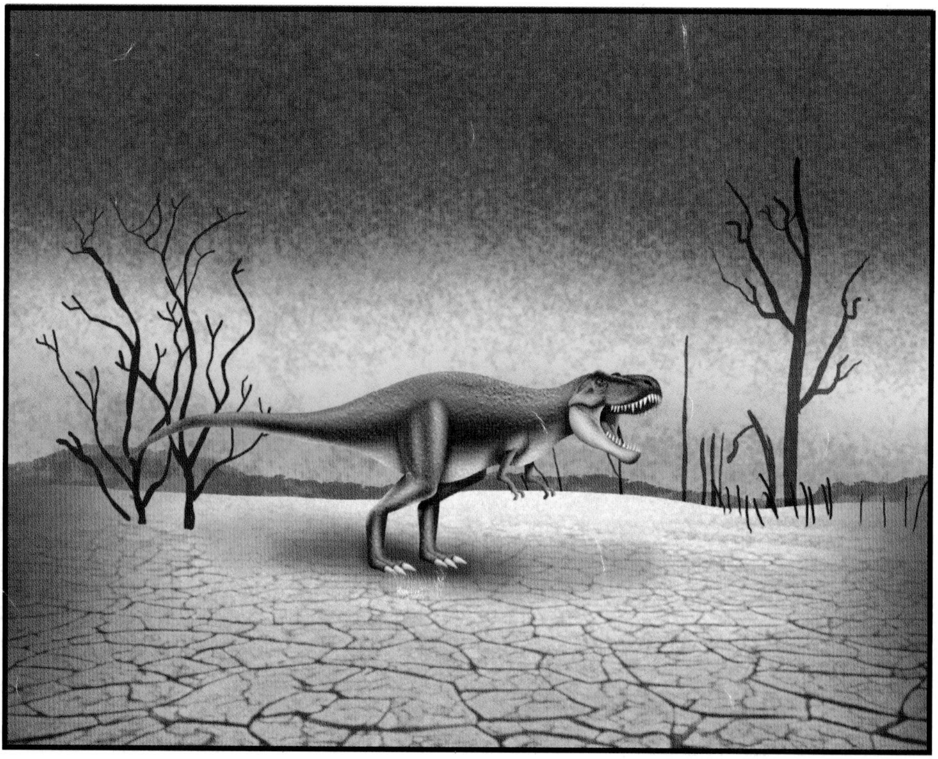

Some scientists think gasses from volcanoes killed the dinosaurs.

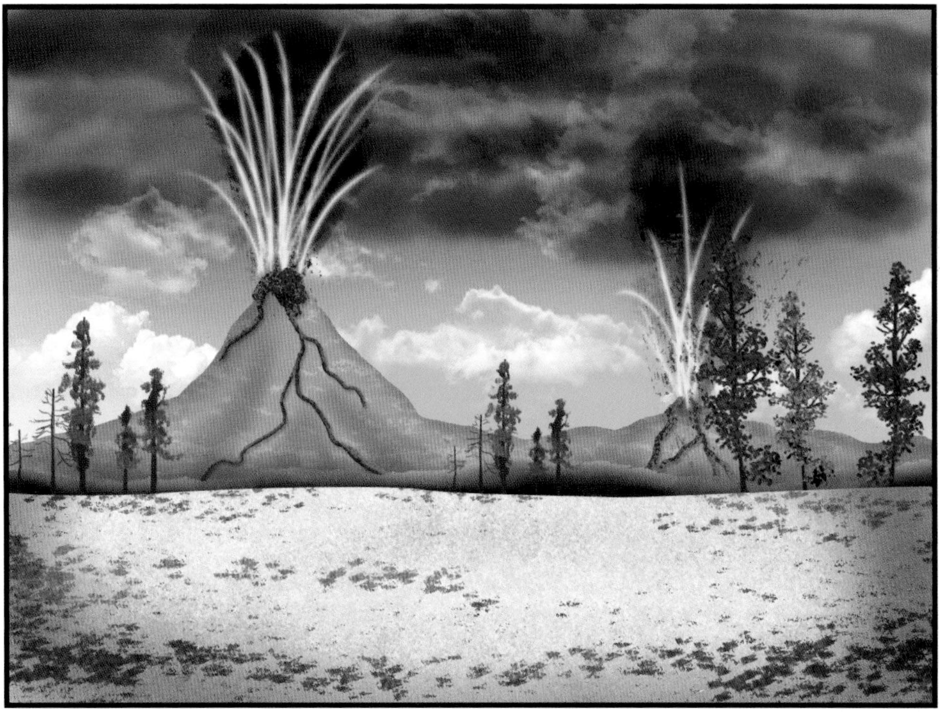

Whatever the reason, T. rex is extinct.

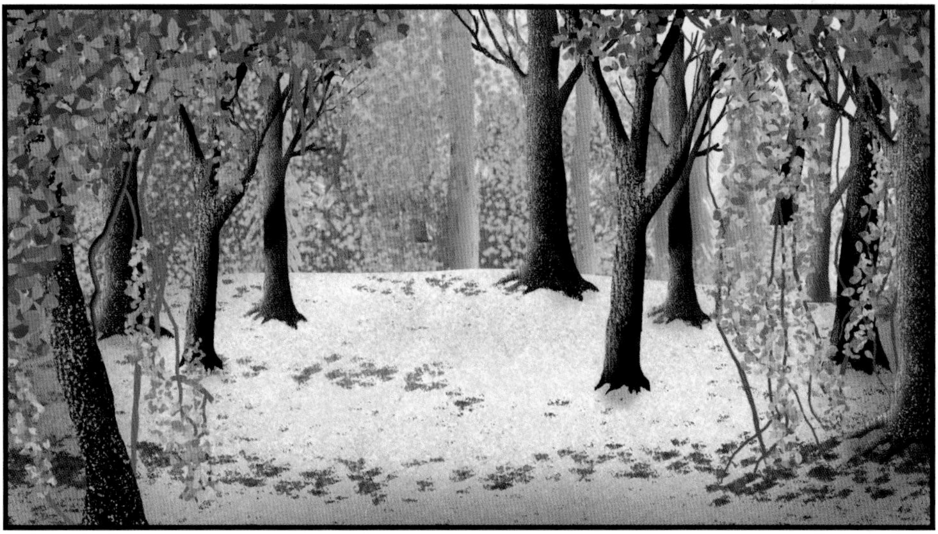

Today T. rex's bones are fossils. Over time, mud and water turned the bones to stone.

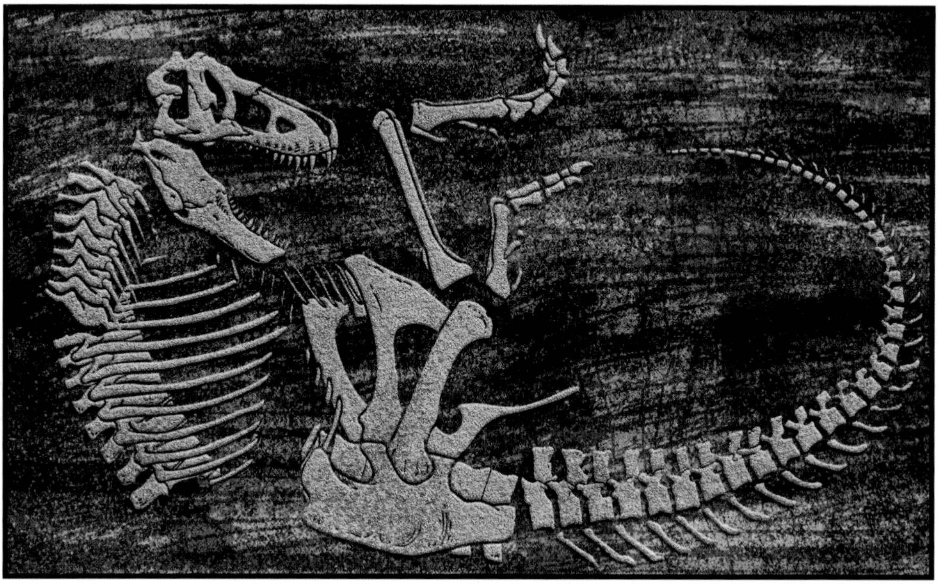

Scientists study the fossils to learn about T. rex.

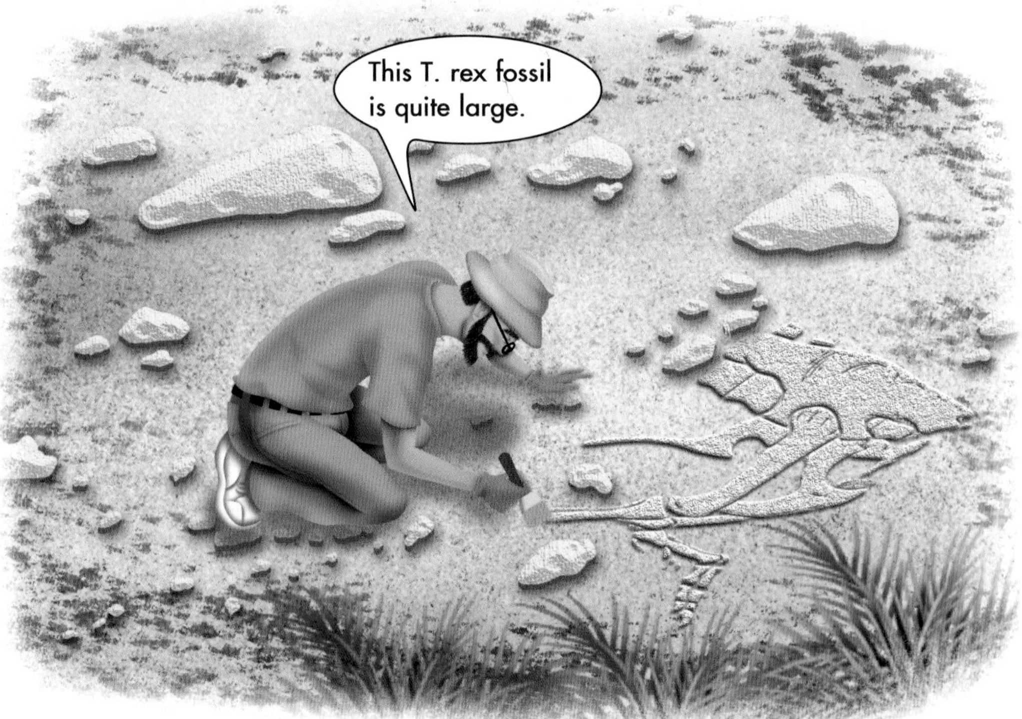
This T. rex fossil is quite large.

Scientists make copies of the bones and put them together. The bones give an idea of what T. rex looked like.

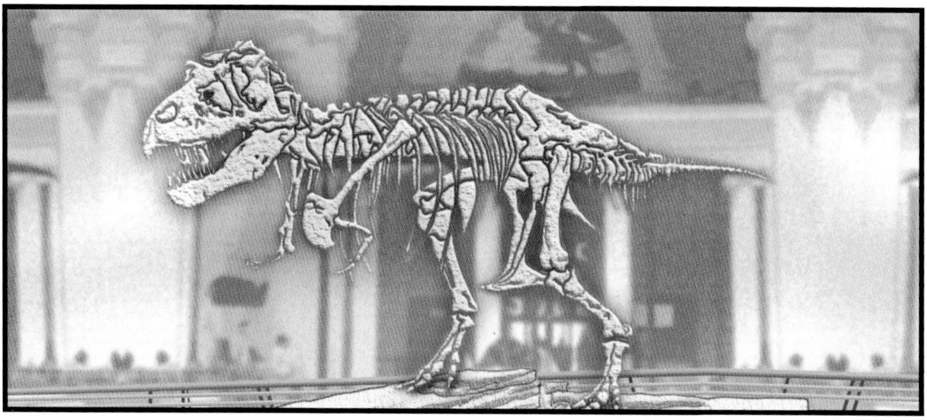

Scientists don't really know what life was like for T. rex. But they continue to study the king of the dinosaurs.

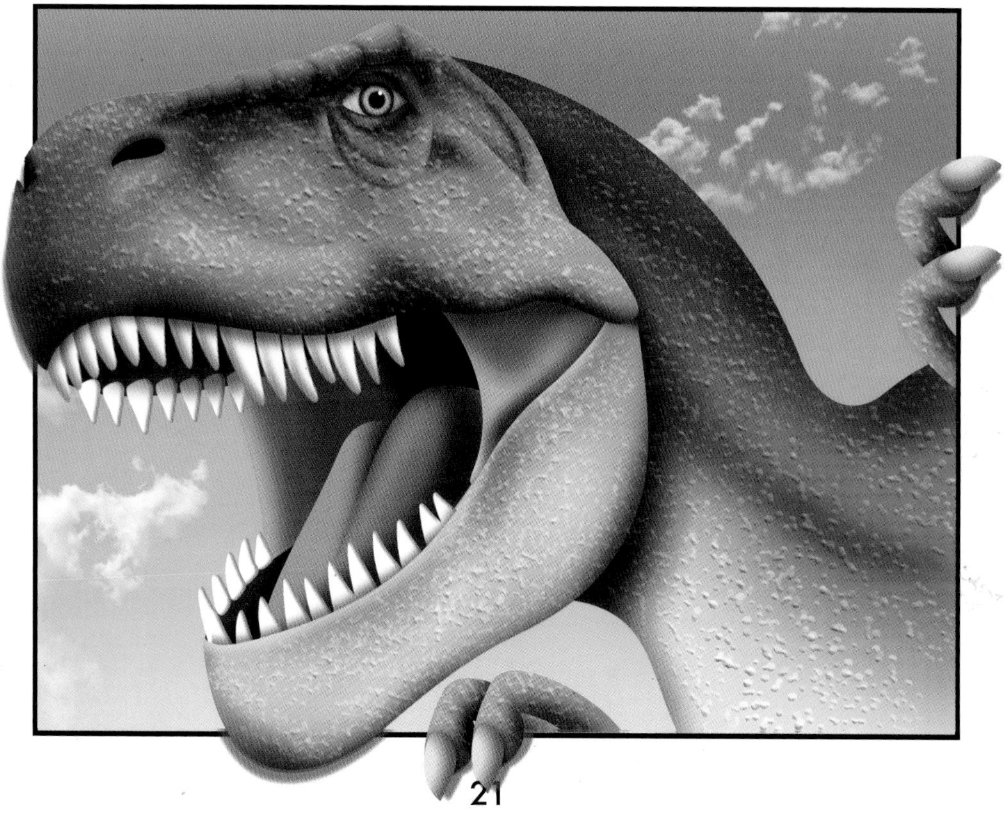

GLOSSARY

extinct—no longer living; an extinct animal is one that has died out, with no more of its kind

fossil—the remains or traces of an animal or a plant, preserved as rock

kill—an animal or animals killed by another animal

meteorite—a large chunk of rock that hits a planet

predator—an animal that hunts other animals for food

prey—an animal hunted by another animal for food

reptile—a cold-blooded animal that breathes air and has a backbone; most reptiles have scales

scavenger—an animal that feeds on animals that are already dead

warm-blooded—having a body temperature that stays about the same all the time

READ MORE

Dodson, Peter. *Tyrannosaurus Rex Up Close: Meat-eating Dinosaur.* Zoom In on Dinosaurs! Berkeley Heights, N.J.: Bailey Books/Enslow Publishers, 2011.

Lee, Sally. *The Pebble First Guide to Dinosaurs.* First Guides. Mankato, Minn.: Capstone Press, 2010.

Pryor, Kimberly Jane. *Tyrannosaurus Rex.* Discovering Dinosaurs. New York: Marshall Cavendish Benchmark, 2012.

INTERNET SITES

FactHound offers a safe, fun way to find Internet sites related to this book. All of the sites on FactHound have been researched by our staff.

Here's all you do:

Visit *www.facthound.com*

Type in this code: 9781429676021

Check out projects, games and lots more at
www.capstonekids.com

INDEX

TITLES IN THIS SET:

Stegosaurus:
Armored Defender

Tyrannosaurus Rex:
Mighty Meat-Eater

Triceratops:
Three-Horned Giant

Velociraptor:
Clawed Hunter

FIRST GRAPHICS

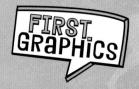

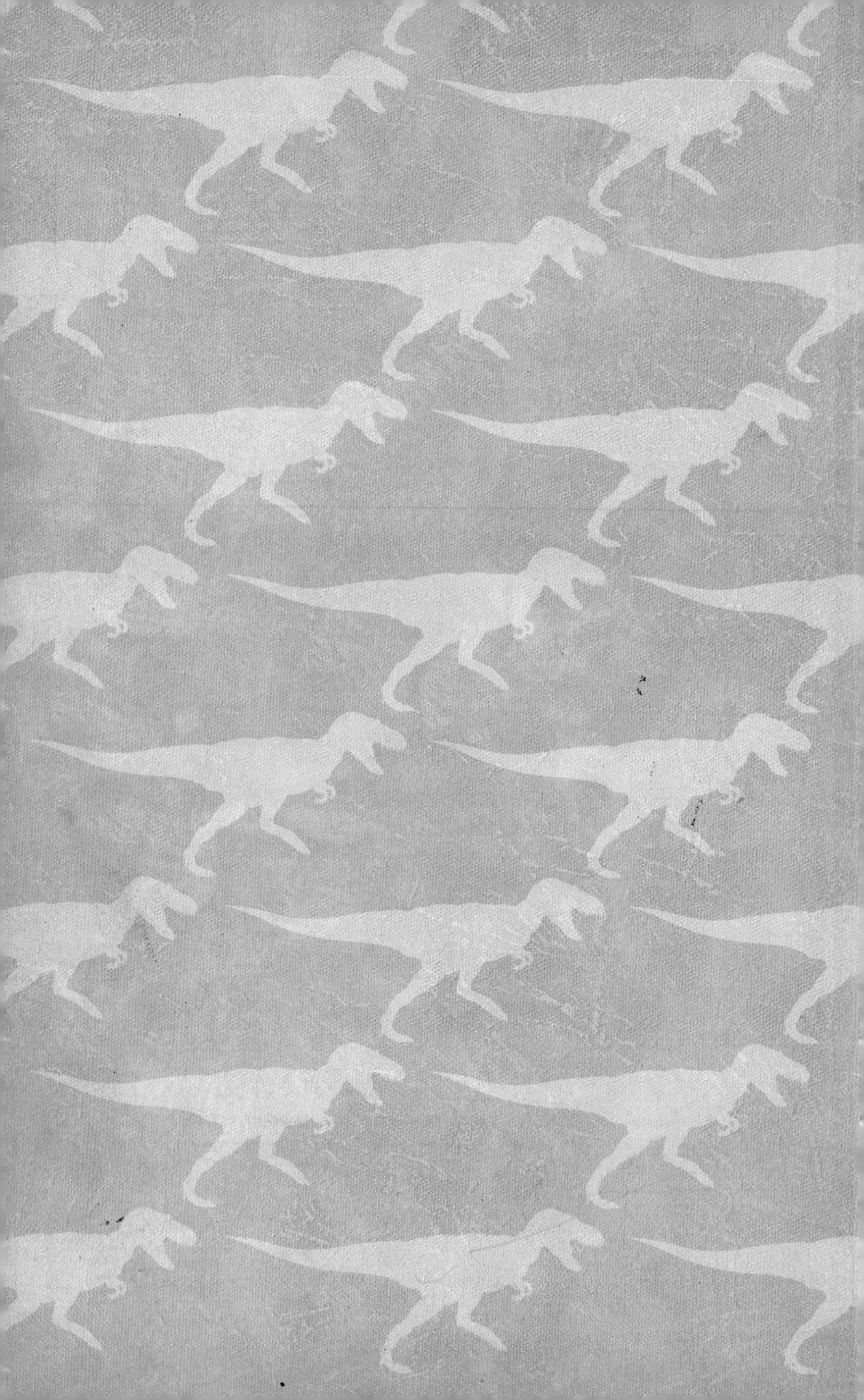